BECAUSE WE CARE

1199 New England Members Tell Their Story

HARD BALL
PRESS

ISBN: 979-8-9898025-2-4

Library of Congress Cataloging-in-Publication Data: Sheard, Timothy

Because We Care – 1199 New England Members Tell Their Story

1. SEIU 1199 2. 1199 New England 3. Certified Nursing Assistant 4. Personal Care Assistant 5. Homecare 6. Nursing Home 7. Hard Ball Press 8. Labor Union

Cover art by Marc Nelson
Book design by Matthew Tallon

Edited by Alma Farnsworth & Timothy Sheard
Set in 13 Gerogia font.
Published by Hardball Press, Brooklyn, New York

www.hardballpress.com

TABLE OF CONTENTS

INTRODUCTION

I love these stories and you will too! The caregivers who opened themselves up by writing about their experiences are remarkable people. It's not just anyone who can do this work, as you will learn. I've gotten to know many, many caregivers in my years as the Executive Director of the 1199 NE Training Fund, and it has given me an appreciation of the love and compassion that they give every day.

The education that we offer at the Training Fund is not only about going to college to get a degree, though many of our members do that every year. Education is also about looking inward, reflecting on our lives, and sharing those reflections with the world in order to make a difference. That's what our members have done in this book.

Thanks also to Tim Sheard and Alma Farnsworth, who have worked countless hours with these writers to help polish up their stories. I know how meaningful this is to the two of them!

Steve Bender, Executive Director, Training & Upgrade Fund

A NOTE FROM AN EDITOR

Take a good look at the hands of a caregiver: the ones who bathe an elderly or disabled client, comb their hair, dress them and take them out into the sunshine. You may see nail polish that is chipped and worn. That is because caregivers use their hands to lift up, to steady, to comfort...to protect and to embrace. These are working hands. Hands that heal.

Take a look at the face of a caregiver. You will see kindness. Respect. Concern. You will see worry and thoughtful planning. You will see humor, and you will see love.

The stories in this little book give readers an opportunity to meet the women and men who care for our most vulnerable. You will learn about their challenges and about their accomplishments. Their journey to care and their everyday tasks.

And in that learning you will grow to love them, as they love the clients they so tenderly embrace.

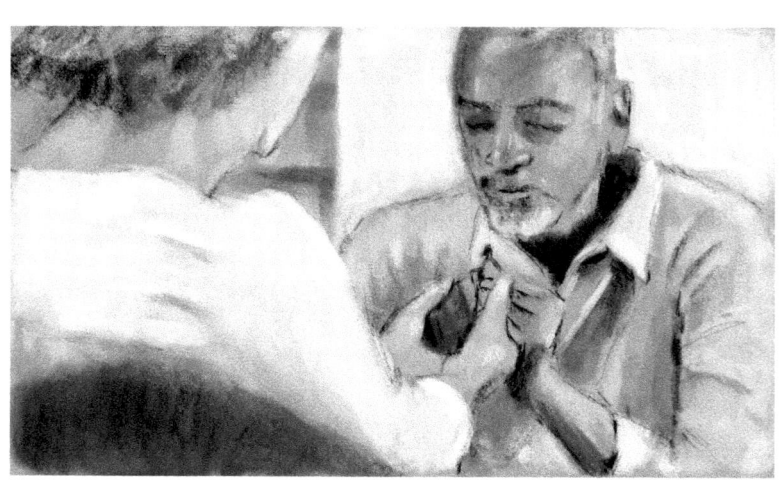

My Spiritual Calling
STEPHEN ARNOLD

Stephen Arnold, Sr. is a dedicated LPN with over 16 years of experience caring for mentally challenged and dementia patients. He is also a certified wound care specialist. He holds a master's degree in counseling psychology from Cambridge College in Massachusetts. Stephen possesses a spiritual calling instilled within him at an early age. Guided by his spiritual principles, he has committed his life to improve the quality of all his patients' lives. He is heavily involved in leadership and teaching at his place of worship. He is also a member of the Trustee Board. He loves to spend time with family and friends.

The journey of my life is reflective now. At 74 years of age, as I look back on my journey through life, I remember that as a young man, certain thoughts, memories, and questions about my spiritual conflict entered my mind. My questions about spirituality that were once conflicting were answered once I accepted my spiritual calling. When I was very young, I accepted what I was to do with my life in the physical world. This calling from God was to use the vocation that was gifted to me, which was to serve and to uplift others.

My father and mother were parents of twelve children, and they raised us in a Christian home. They taught us Christian living and exemplified a Christian lifestyle. Our family was blessed with prosperity and spirituality, and our family never lacked for anything in our lives. Our father truly believed and practiced the biblical doctrine, which maintains that every father is to take care of his family by providing spiritual guidance, nurturance, and financial security to meet the family needs. My father's work ethics, parenting skills, and his duty to provide for the family were his core values. I learned this from him. With the acceptance of my spiritual calling, the indwelling of the Holy Spirit is directing my life's decisions and convincing me to dutifully accept and continue allowing this Holy Spirit to lead my life.

I recall the days when I attended seventh and eighth grade. I enjoyed spending time in the library. While there, I really found peace when I researched about Christianity in the encyclopedias. These are still my fondest memories. I really enjoyed reading about the Christian Wars and tried to understand the stories. Also, during that time, on Sunday mornings my father usually called on me to read Bible verses during our family Bible study in our home. Reading the Bible was important to me. I felt special and acknowledged.

In my teens, my father would take me in the car with him to attend Fellowship with other churches. He was a church elder, and I will always remember and cherish my experiences of one-on-one time with him. And my wonderful mother! She treated me so "special." She always took me grocery and clothes shopping with her, and we visited church members at their homes. She prophesied about future events in my life. Several times, privately, she would say, "Steve, my spirit does not feel right, stay in the house tonight." Every time she said that to me, sure enough, her spirit was correct.

On one occasion when she felt that I should stay home, on the very next day, I heard the sad news that a person that my mother called her "son' was arrested for burglary. I was thankful for God's manifestation that He had revealed to my mother. And strangely enough, I recall another specific event in my life when I was led by the divine spirit to not go to a party. I learned the next day that a neighbor, who lived down the street from me, had been stabbed. He survived, but I still have the feeling, "What if I had gone?"

My mother was so peaceful when she spoke to me; I rarely heard her raise her voice to any of her children. She was a Godly woman who was involved in the church in which we were members. She taught us so much. Cooking was very important to her and our family. She would have all her children around the stove to show us how to cook. She would take her time to explain the ingredients and amount of time needed to prepare and then cook the food. Then, a prayer was said before we ate each meal. Usually, the prayer of thanks was for the blessings that God bestowed on our family.

Initially, as a young man, I was afraid of the calling that God had placed in my soul. My conscience was at war with my spiritual calling and my worldly desires. In high school, I felt out of place. There were more than a thousand students there, and it was overwhelming for me. I assumed that everyone was raised as I was raised in a two-parent, Christian-based home. I played on the basketball team and the football team, but after practice and the games, most all the other team members engaged in conversations that were not in line with how I was raised. My spirit was troubled, and I soon realized that I could not conform to this kind of group.

This group always talked negatively about the girls in school, and their derogatory comments were offensive to me. I have four sisters that I love dearly, and their conversations made me upset. I was taught to respect and honor women. So, when I listened to my teammates' insulting conversations about females, I attempted to engage in helpful conversation, but it fell on deaf ears. I ventured out to join other groups, but the results were the same. My spiritual calling remained the same, and the purpose that God had intended for me was to lead others to their calling that God had for them.

As I matured into adulthood, I pressed forward with my spiritual calling. I went to school to become an LPN. My work in the medical field as an LPN in a nursing rehabilitation center is very rewarding. The rewards I receive are from using the spiritual gift of helping others, which far outweighs the monetary rewards of a paycheck. I realize now that my primary calling is not connected to my employer, but it is primarily connected to what God has called me to do. My calling is to use God's gift to care for humankind in this world.

I used my spiritual gifts by praying silently and verbally for my patients and residents in nursing facilities and others at the church that I attend. I pray for peace and well-being for humankind all over the world. Some people request prayer for medical healing. In the nursing facilities, many male and female residents in their transitional stage of life ask that I pray for them and hold their hand. Other residents during their end stage of life have asked me, "Please forgive me for being mean to you." I told them, "Yes, I forgive you." But, just as God has forgiven me, I already had forgiven them on the day of the occurrence.

As a member of the church under the direction of our pastor, I was assigned leadership roles. I did not expect to become the Adult Men Sunday School teacher, but I was assigned to this role through the manifestation of the Holy Spirit that was revealed to my Pastor. God provided the necessary gifts to allow me to teach the unaltered Word of God to the men at our church. Dutifully, through God's grace and the supplier of all my needs to carry out His mission for me, I was assigned more tasks. To be a servant for Christ is rewarding, and it gives me a purpose and fulfillment of my soul. Currently, I am on the finance committee and have financial duties that I am entrusted to fulfill.

Ever since the Covid Epidemic, my involvement in

doing work in the ministry is continuing to grow in understanding and application of the Bible Scriptures. During that 18- month period when no physical contact was allowed, I was asked by my pastor to teach a telephone conference call to the congregation. I believe God used me at that time for preparation for His plan and purpose for my life, and I am accepting it in the belief of His divine power that is orchestrating my life. I am being used by God more and more. I believe that the Lord's spirit works through others who are leaders and united in the Holy Spirit throughout the world. I am being used to help others to accept their calling that God has for them, and when I teach the Word of God over the congregation, I am accepting Gods' calling over my life. The joy that I get from doing the will of God creates a peaceful atmosphere in our home. Prayer is important, and I lead corporate prayer in our Church. At our home, my wife and I pray daily in the start of our day, and afterwards, we read a Bible scriptures, and this keeps our union grounded in faith in our Lord.

My purposeful studying of the Bible fulfils and enriches my spirit, and the feelings and words in my heart manifest in my behavior so that I can offer much love for humanity, forgiveness, sympathy and acceptance of others. I am truly blessed with my spiritual calling, and I find great fulfillment in my life. I have been gifted with great satisfaction, pleasure, and comfort. I feel great relief that my God-gifted talents and abilities can help others find their place in this world or save their lives at the nursing facilities where I use God's gift of caring for others in this world. This spiritual calling gives me a deep sense to know what I am meant to do with my God-given life in the physical world. This spiritual calling is my mission and purpose in my life. I know that God's calling for me is serving, helping, and saving others. I know in my soul what I am meant to do.

John 3:31-36-: The one from Heaven

31-The one who comes from above is above all. The one who is from earth is earthy and speaks in earthy terms. The one who comes from heaven is above all. **32**-He testifies to what he has seen and heard and yet no one accepts his testimony. **33**-The one who accepted his testimony has affirmed that God is true. **34**- For the one whom God sent speaks God's words since he gives the spirit without measure. **35**- The father loves the Son and has given all things into his hands. **36**-The One who believes in the Son has eternal life, but the one who rejects the Son will not see life; instead, the wrath of God remains on him.

Verses 31-32 Jesus– the one—- is the Son of God speaking from heavenly perspective.

Verse 36- Jesus will one day rule the world as King, thus believe in the Son to receive eternal life.

Your Journey In Life
ROMONA BARNES

Romona Barnes became a CNA right out of high school in 1986, and she started as a CNA at Waterbury Hospital. Concurrently, she worked at the hospital and as a CNA at Whitewood Rehabilitation Center and later other nursing facilities in Connecticut. During the hospital transition to all PCAs, Romona earned her certification in EKG and Phlebotomy and continued working at the hospital. Currently, she is working as a CNA at the Waterbury Center for Nursing and Rehabilitation. Patients and staff alike say she is a strong and valued leader, and she takes exceptional care of her patients as she would any family member. For the past 34 years, she has been an 1199 SEIU New England Union lead delegate at the Waterbury Hospital, where she proudly advocates for what is best for her fellow union members and hospital patients. Romona has three grown sons, and her youngest works in radiology and plans to be a doctor. In her spare time, she sings in her church choir and spends time with her three grandchildren. She is also an excellent baker.

Sometimes you don't know where your journey in life will take you.

I walked into the patient's room. The air was a little funky. You know- that nursing home urine smell. I walked in a little closer to the bed where there lay a little Italian woman. I didn't really know how to pronounce her name, so I reached out and touched the off-white flannel blanket that was covering her and said, "Mrs. Coldiani, I'm here to get you washed up."

As she turned to look at me, I added, "My name is Romona."

She corrected me and said her name is "Coliani."

I said, "Okay. Can I get you cleaned up and up to your chair for breakfast?"

She nodded 'yes.' I pulled the covers back to see this frail little body. You could see her veins through her paper-thin skin. As I pulled her closer to the edge of the bed, you could hear her bones cracking. Her silver hair had fallen down around her face, so I told her I would fix her hair in the bathroom.

She started walking slowly towards the bathroom, her bones cracking again. I kept reassuring her she was all right, and I still pronounced her name wrong.

I finally got her into the bathroom, where I washed her

up with baby bubble bath and warm water (it leaves the skin smelling really nice). When she was dry, I dressed her in a beautiful blue, printed snap back dress and a baby blue sweater.

I asked Mrs. Coliani to sit still while I went to get her hairbrush. I started brushing her hair, which was a very pretty silver and white mix. I put up her hair in a little bun with a blue hair comb that she had on her bedside table.

Stepping back to look her over, I asked how she felt now that she was cleaned and dressed? She just smiled, saying nothing. I walked with her back to her living space and helped her settle in her recliner. Then I told her that breakfast will be coming soon. She said, "Thank you."

A little later I came back to bring her breakfast. It really wasn't much to talk about. It was a pureed diet and everything looked like slop. She really ate only the oatmeal. In between her sips of coffee and orange juice, she told me that I was a beautiful lady.

Mrs. Coliani was my first patient. She was the reason that made me want to care for the elderly. I had taken the time to care for her, this mother, grandmother, sister and friend. She gave me the opportunity to care for her and make her comfortable when she needed it the most.

I came back to her room later that morning, a little close to noon, and asked if she needed anything else. I went to touch her, but she did not respond. I called out her name, "Mrs. Coliani! *Mrs Coliani!*"

But she made no answer. Mrs. Coliani had slowly slipped away. My eyes watered up and my heart broke into pieces. She had touched me more than I had even realized, and she changed my course in caring for the elderly. I learned from her about giving love, showing compassion and empathy, and just listening-something that we all want.

And that we all truly need.

I Care Deeply

JENNIFER BENNETT

Jennifer Bennett began her lessons in the art of compassionate caregiving when she was very young, while taking care of her mother in Jamaica. Jennifer came to the United States, where she became a CNA and raised her two sons. For over 7 years she has embraced the challenges and rewards that come with her patient care role. For her, going the extra mile to ensure that her patients feel loved, appreciated, and respected is paramount. Jennifer is continuing her education to earn her associate's degree in business administration management. One of her sons has recently graduated with his BS in engineering, and her other son is now working as an architectural draftsman. Jennifer has been an 1199 Union delegate for two years and is dedicated to being an advocate for her fellow Union members. She volunteers at her church, and in her free time she enjoys singing, sewing, baking and spending time with her family.

At a young age, I was immersed in the profound lessons of caregiving. Growing up in Jamaica, my mother became ill with a degenerative disease. I was thirteen. Over time the illness affected her mobility. As her condition worsened, I began to learn about managing the house, and more importantly, I began to learn the art of compassionate care. It was physically tiring. However, the lessons in being a caring support for my mom had a great impact on my life. They were lessons in love, compassion, and support for another human. These experiences fueled my decision to become a caregiver and to embrace the challenges and rewards that come with the role.

In 2013, I migrated to the United States with my family. I soon earned my certification as a nursing assistant, then worked first in home care and later in a nursing home facility.

Several years after becoming a CNA I met a special lady. It was on a cold and snowy winter afternoon that I met Ms. Gee, an elderly Jamaican lady who had recently moved to my nursing home. She had medium length silver-gray hair, and her dark skin revealed wrinkles that were formed around her forehead, neck, and hands. Upon her arrival at the nursing home, Ms. Gee seemed extremely quiet and apprehensive, sitting in her wheelchair keenly observing her new surroundings with questionable eyes. Ms. Gee's facial expression was always somber.

I walked over to greet her. After introducing myself, I asked her name. She paused for a moment or two, then looked at me with a keen stare and frankly responded,

"Wah yuh waan fi kno mi name fah? Yuh mada neva tell yuh nuh chat tuh strangas?" (To translate in English, she meant, "Why do you want to know my name. Your mother did not tell you not to talk to strangers?")

Hearing her Jamaican vernacular, I replied, "Oh! I see you are a Jamaican. Where in Jamaica are you from?" I informed her that I, too, was from Jamaica, but Ms. Gee had no interest in our shared background. Instead she further stated, "Yuh too fass dat a mi business." ("You're too inquisitive of my concern") Her reluctance to be engaged was obvious. Ms. Gee had been living alone for years and seemed eager to return to the only home she had known for years.

The following day, I entered her room with a warm greeting. Despite her initial resistance, I found joy in helping her choose her clothes and preparing her for the day. As we went through our morning routine, I whispered Jamaican songs I thought would be familiar to her, and to my delight, she started humming along. Before long, we were both singing and giggling with each other. Our morning routine became a small ritual, during which she began with a twinkle in her eyes to share stories of her past, which included her favorite memory of our birth island–Jamaica. Each time she shared a story, the joy and nostalgia that was shown in her eyes were noticeable and priceless!

Naturally, she also wanted me to share my story, to which I would remind her of our first meeting, and jokingly used her own words against her, stating, "But look, yuh waan fass ina mi business now?" (Now, you're the one who is being inquisitive/interested in my affairs/concerns?) She knew I was joking and grinned from ear to ear.

Oftentimes, her words became disorganized and erratic as we conversed, which regularly reminded me of her frail mind and onset dementia. Although Ms. Gee's mind was slowly fading, I would do everything in my power to preserve the spark she had, with the same care and attention I had for my mother.

Caring for Ms. Gee was not just about helping with her daily personal care, but also about celebrating her rich life and preserving her dignity. Going the extra mile to ensure that she felt loved, appreciated, valued, heard, and happy was paramount to me. This is evident in the small, thoughtful gestures we make daily as caregivers. Whether it's lending a listening ear, offering support, or making the time to share in their memories, our care shines as a beacon of hope and connection, and those were my genuine concerns for Ms. Gee, because I deeply care.

My Dad

BEATRICE BOANSI

Beatrice Boansi was born in Ghana. She came to the United States in 1990. Beatrice has three children - two girls and one boy, and she has one grandson. Beatrice has been working as a CNA for the last 20 years. She currently works at Fresh River Health Care in East Windsor, CT.

Beatrice has been an 1199 NE delegate for several years, where she advocates for her co-workers and for the union.

I loved my dad.

My dad had two names. One name was Yaw Asae. The other name was Yaw Anyinam, which means "Light." I like the latter one better.

He was a professional driver. He was very cautious about the way he drove. He owned a Mercedes Benz wagon that could hold about 35 passengers.

People used to line up the night before the next travel day to load their goods on his bus. If they did not load them the night before, there would be no room for them in the morning, his trips were so popular.

What I love the most about my dad, if you may ask, is the fact that he got up so very early in the morning to go to work. As a result, we never saw him until the evening rolled in. And we were *so* glad to have him home!

My dad had a quotation in front of his wagon that said, "Show your love." Because we never saw our dad in the morning before he left for work, he made sure on his day off that we had his undivided attention.

And his love.

When he arrived back in town from his run, before he dropped off his passengers, he would blow his horn to alert us that he was coming home soon. The sound of the horn was between him and us, it was our secret signal.

On his day off he would lay out a long table in the house compound and he would lay out all kinds of delicacies for us to enjoy. Now mind you, these were African dishes, and still are to this day.

The food consisted of kenkay, which is made of fermented cornmeal wrapped in corn husks and cooked for hours to perfection. Another kenkey has the same ingredients, except this was wrapped in green plantain leaves that gave an authentic aroma. That was my dad's favorite. Other delicacies included fried fish, shrimp, and canned sardines that were mashed with peppers, tomatoes, onions and shrimp sauce. It's called black pepper kenkey.

My dad also reared chickens, goats, sheep, and ducks. So when Christmas came, we had a blast.

What else can I say about my dad? If you had a problem, he was the go-to guy. I don't know if I should call this a jokes or a theory (my dad had plenty of both!), but in his older years when his eyes sight was dimming he claimed that the doctor had shone a bright light in his eyes, and that was what caused his eye problems. Another "theory" was, any doctor that stops him from eating salt does know what they're doing.

**

My dad was very handsome. Very tall, too. Back in the day, corporal punishment was the norm. If we did something wrong and my mom wanted him to punish us, he would take us to the side and just give us a slap on the tush. My mom thought that just was not right, but we were happy.

My dad was a very principled man. His "yes" meant "yes" and his "no" meant "No way!"

Until my dad died, I had no idea that he was a union leader for his fellow drivers and was respected by so many of them. But as life goes, one day I got a call that he wasn't feeling well, and before I could buy a ticket to go see him, since I hadn't been home in around five years, word came back that he had passed and we didn't need to rush down.

His passing left a hole in my heart. But time heals all wounds. I had wanted to be able to take care of him like I do for my patients here in the US, but that never came to fruition. Still, he knew how much I loved him, and I knew how much he kept me in his heart.

An Unexpected Outcome
JUDY DOYLE

Judy Doyle is a dedicated professional with over 20 years of experience in education. She holds a master's degree in educational leadership and is committed to providing personal support for adults with special needs. Judy is also passionate about writing, channeling her creativity and insights into her work and personal projects.

It was early in the afternoon when we left for the airport. The sky was clear and the air was crisp—a perfect day to fly. So, we started on our journey to Poland.

We made idle chat as we drove to JFK Airport in New York, discussing where we were going, what we were going to see, and what to expect when we landed in another country. It was the first trip for my mother and me to take together, and it was a long time coming—forty-nine years to be exact.

Who knows if we will get to do it again? But for now, the adventure was upon us, and that was all that mattered. I was thrilled to be getting out of the country once again.

As we pulled into the parking lot at JFK, that feeling of excitement overcame me. "Wow, we are actually doing this!" I said.

My mom was clueless about what was going to happen next. She said, "What do we do now? Where do we go?"

We found a parking space near the train. We parked in Lot B, far from the other cars but close enough so the walk wouldn't be too bad. As we made our way to the airport, we passed all sorts of people, coming and going. I love people-watching, so airports are entertaining for me. We met a lovely couple on their way to a wedding in Italy. We spoke to them for a few minutes as we waited for security. The security line was ridiculously long. It went all the way down the hall and around the corner. It took about 40 minutes. They really should figure out a better way to check people and bags. Once we got past security, we headed to our terminal. It was packed, but we had about an hour before we boarded, so we stopped for a little snack. We had yummy dumplings and $20 water. If you have ever been to an airport, you know the prices for things are just outrageous—the old supply and demand. We know you can't bring it into the airport, so they charge you triple for the convenience of offering you something you can get at the store for only two dollars. JFK gets over 26 million people through its doors every year, so they have a good racket going on.

When we finished our snack, we headed back to the terminal, found seats, and I started charging my phone. I wasn't sure what to expect on the flight, so I wanted to be prepared. As my phone was charging, I went over to the window to check out the plane. It was a double-decker. If my partner Chris were here, he would have told me all about the plane—the type, the speed, how many passengers. All I know is I was excited to be flying on my first double-decker. No wonder the terminal had so many passengers. Next time I fly international, I'm going up top.

We settled into our seats. We sat in the middle of the plane, behind the stewardess station and bathrooms, so we had no seats in front of us. It took us a while to figure out where the screens were and how to get comfortable. I sat on the outside of the middle row, and Mom sat right next to me. The seats were pretty comfortable, and the movie selection was pretty good, so I quickly found a movie and started watching. However, my mother had different plans and continued to talk. We talked about our expectations and what it would be like during the visit. On international flights, you get free drinks, so the first thing they ask for is drinks, then dinner. Dinner was pretty good, which surprised me.

After dinner, it was getting late, and I thought I would try to sleep, so I put on a movie and tried sleeping. You can never get really comfortable on a plane, so I tossed and turned all flight. When we finally landed in Germany, it was still dark out, but you could see the sun starting to rise. We had to go through customs and get our passports stamped, but luckily, it was so early we were the only ones, and we were through in minutes. We didn't have a long layover, which was good because not many places were open when we arrived. We got these horrible boiled sausage things and a drink. I didn't remember the food being this bad the last time I was in Germany, but Mom and I ate and then headed to our gate. Before we knew it, we were on our way to Wrocław. This plane was small, with two seats on each side and only about 50 passengers. The engine was loud. I tried closing my eyes to get a little rest before our adventure began. It seemed to work, because we were on the ground in no time.

When we got off the plane, my older half-brother was waiting for us. We were exhausted from traveling all night but excited and exhilarated at the same time, so sleep was not on the agenda. Instead, we piled into his truck and headed into Wrocław. We first stopped at this big store to pick up cement for my brother's outside shower. The store was like a Home Depot/Ikea mix, and huge. My mom and I both tried to figure out the costs of everything because the prices were a little lower. John told us to divide everything by four, and that's the American cost, so if it was 100 zloty, it was 25 American dollars. It was awesome, and I used it to my advantage a few times on our trip.

Our first day, we went on a boat ride around the city, seeing and listening to the history of Wrocław and seeing all the wonders of another country. We had delicious food—Mexican and yummy drinks—before we headed back to John's apartment to meet his wife Iza and my nephew Matie. Matie reminded me of my brother when he was little with all the freckles. He had long curly hair on the top, and my brother had short hair, but they had the same features. I don't think either looked like my mom. My mom is Italian with dark hair and brown eyes, the total opposite.

We went all over Poland exploring the first couple of days. The Poland zoo had animals I had not seen before, like the okapi. The salt caves were amazing. The labor that went into digging the tunnels and creating all the salt structures—you just have to be in awe and amazement.

My favorite place was Zakopane. It was a small ski town and had lots of shops and open markets to explore. We had a delicious lunch on a rooftop and a late dinner that was just as divine. However, breakfast was not my favorite. I like my pierogi fried, and this plum-boiled pierogi was just not my style.

The next day, my brother convinced us to walk to the base of the mountain. He said it was a short trip. What a load of bull that was. Sure, it wasn't a *long* walk, but it was all *uphill!* When we finally got to the top, my mom and I rested while they stood in line, and then we all decided we didn't want to wait the two hours for the gondola ride to the top. We headed back down and decided to go to the other mountain. On the way down, we all put our feet in the stream and joked about how cold the water was, while my brother John was like, "This is nothing." As a Wim Hof instructor (a discipline that teaches you the power of the breath and cold as a natural path to strength and health), he is used to the cold water. We joked and laughed and had a grand old time on the way back to the hotel.

We stopped at the hotel for a quick nap, and then we were off to the other side of the gondola. My mom and I were chatting and commenting on the great time we were having and how we had done more steps than ever before. When we got to the top of the mountain, we enjoyed the breathtaking views of the mountains and valleys. John pointed out the parts he had hiked, while Matie skateboarded all around the area. We rode back just as the sun was setting and enjoyed another delicious snack while we soaked up each other's company and the spectacular vacation we were having.

The next day, we drove back to Wroclaw. It was a long drive. We stopped at my brother's friend's winery for a tour before we headed back to the apartment. Four or more hours later, we were back. With only a few more days of vacation left, we shopped, visited my brother's log house outside the city, met Iza's family for a delicious homemade pizza dinner, and just enjoyed the time I had with the family and my mom.

When it was time to leave, we said our goodbyes, thanked them for a great time, and packed the truck to leave for the airport. At the airport, I quickly did some shopping for everyone back home and took pictures of this adorable gremlin at the airport. My mom and I talked about how amazed we were with the trip and how it exceeded our expectations. It was just the right amount of time.

The flight home was uneventful, and when we finally landed, went through customs, and got home, it was around midnight. This trip changed my relationship with my mom. We relied on each other, worked as a team, and survived a week together without once fighting. It was a life-changing experience and one my mom and I will cherish always.

My Moment of Connection
GLORIA DUQUETTE

Gloria Duquette has worked for many years as a CNA, where she gives her love and tenderness to all her clients. Gloria is also an active leader in her Union, advocating for her members and bringing union news to the rank and file.

My moment of connection begins in a small town in Jamaica where I was born and grew up. I came into this world the daughter of older parents because before me, their child, my brother, was mentally retarded. So, after he died my mom and dad decided to try for another child, and I soon was born.

As soon as I was old enough to handle responsibilities, I began to take care of my aging parents, as well as take care of my child, me being a single mother. All my life I have been giving to others what was needed. It might be registering people to vote, or putting on school events, or organizing Christmas tree celebrations for the children, although I did *not* put on a Santa Claus beard!

I moved to this country and started working in the health field as a nurse's assistant. I love doing what I am doing. I get to meet all different types of people from all walks of life, and I enjoy every day that I go to work.

One moment that stuck with me was when I was working in a nursing home in Simsbury, Connecticut. A beautiful, petite patient by the name of Adele was admitted. She had beautiful silvery hair and sad eyes. She came in with her sons and her daughter-in-law. I went to her room, greeted her and her family and told her, "I am your aide on the 3-11 shift."

About 15 minutes later a family member came out of the room and called to me, saying, "Can you please come back, because she is just crying and crying."

I walked back and entered the room. The patient was sitting on the bed crying very hard. I sat beside her and hugged her. Adele turned to me and held me so tight. I started to rock her and whisper in her ear, "You are safe, now. You are safe with me."

She wept and wept and wept. I then realized, it was her family members being there–that was why she was so upset. I said to one of her sons, "Would you give me a minute and wait outside, please?"

They left without saying a word.

I continued to hug Adele. I told her, "You are safe, I got you."

She told me, "I am seventy-five years old. I have never been sick, and now they want to throw me away in hell." She started crying again, and I hugged her tighter. She cried for about an hour.

I sat on the side of the bed and gently told Adele, "Do not worry about a thing, I will make sure you are okay. Nothing bad will happen to you here. You are still young."

She said, "You will?"

I told her," Yes, you've got my word."

She asked me to tell her family that she was okay. I went out and told the family, "She's doing okay, but she is a little upset, can I have your number? I will call you later to tell you how she is going on." They understood that she did not want to stay in the home and that she was scared of this strange new environment.

Later in the shift, Adele told me what made her so upset. The poor woman had just lost her husband. They had gone to the hospital for him to take a stress test. All "routine," the doctor had said.

After the test, which seemed to go all right, she went to get the car. When she had brought the car around to the entrance, she saw the hospital staff rushing around her husband, who was lying on the floor in the lobby. He had coded and suffered a cardiac arrest.

Sadly, he died there in the hospital.

After hearing her story, I wrote a note to the social worker explaining about Adele's terribly sad story.

31

When the social worker understood Adele's story, she knew how to care for her: how to make her feel at home and how to begin the long journey of grieving for her lost husband.

When I came back to work the next day at 3 PM, Adele hugged me and said, "Thank you so very much for caring, you were my guardian angel."

Adele stayed in the home for three months, and then she went home. I went to her home and cared for her at night: I was her night companion, until she sold her house and moved away.

I will keep her in my thoughts and in my heart forever.

A Rose Is a Rose

MARGARET ROSE FOLSOM

Margaret Rose Folsom is a PCA/CNA who provides loving care to clients in Stratford, Guilford, Bradford and other towns across the state. Known as Rose, she also works for the 1199 NE Health Care Union. Her most treasured assignments are hospice care, which she provides in the home and in the hospital. Rose also loves to teach the Bible online and at churches across Connecticut.

I am the proud namesake of my aunt, Margaret Rose Folsom, who graduated from Edward Waters College of Nursing. Like Aunt Rose, I have cared for those who needed assistance since I was in kindergarten. You see, Mr. Willie, a neighbor of ours, had an accident on the railroad where he worked. The accident put a hole in his left leg. My mother, who also cared for neighbors, would take me with her to Mr. Willie's house, where she changed his gauze dressing. I saw how she applied iodine to the wound to prevent an infection setting in.

Mr. Willie's wife Miss Ophelia would put me up on a stool to wash dishes. I carried out other chores around the house, and I went to the neighborhood store, Crazy Corner, to pick up snuff tobacco for Mr. Willie.

While caring for Mr. Willie I had to watch The Price is Right, and the television News at noon, followed by The Young and Restless. It was quite an education for a little girl!

When the ice cream truck came down the street, its bell ringing loudly, I was sent to buy butter pecan ice cream. That was Mr. Willie's and Opehlia's favorite flavor.

I got to liking it, too.

It seems that as a child I was always giving care to others. Mrs. Boswell lived behind my building. She had only one hand due to an accident. The neighborhood kids were afraid of her and thought she was mean, because she yelled at us if we went into her yard to get our ball that had flown over her fence. We had to break through branches in the hedge to get to the ball, and that upset her.

Sometimes Mrs. Boswell came to babysit for me when my mother had to go out to work, so I got to know her quite well. I used to rub Bengay on her knees, which were always dry and cracked. Often, she let me pick pecans from her yard where they fell from the trees there. I helped hang her clothes on the backyard line, and I went to Crazy Corner to get Beechnut chewing tobacco for her.

Mrs. Boswell taught me to drink coffee with a cup and saucer. *Very* ladylike. She baked pound cakes, so her house always smelled of sweet cakes and coffee, laced with the minty smell of the Bengay.

Or Absorbine Jr.

Next door to Mrs. Boswell there lived a Mr. Croffet. They had a big black car. And they had a dog that got sick with the mange. I would pick a certain weed that grew around the back yard. Mrs. Croffet would boil the leaves and treat the dog's coat. It smelled pretty bad.

When it was time for them to go to the grocery store, my job was to read the labels and the coupon prices. Mrs. Croffet made bread pudding with peaches. And of course, pecan pie with nuts from Mrs. Boswell's yard

This was my life until I was eleven years old. I grew up in a neighborhood of elderly people, who cared for me just as much as I cared for them.

Ms. Ophelia took me to church for the first time. I came home sick with the mumps. Another time when I had stepped on a toothpick, Mrs. Boswell held me down with her one arm to assist my mother to take it out. I learned about removing foreign objects from a body and how to make bread pudding with peaches.

I didn't get to make pecan pie, though.

In 2006 I became a PCA companion. I cared for Ms. Harper. She was 86 years old when I began working for her. My job was to watch Bonanza, with Little Joe and Horse. We watched Chuck Norris, Walker Texas Ranger, Wheel of Fortune. Then I became her homemaker. I went grocery shopping, picked up her prescriptions, and did some light cleaning and cooking.

Ms. Harper was so sweet. She lived alone and had to stop driving. She didn't like that at all. When I would knock on her door you could hear her say, "Thank you, Jesus, thank you, Jesus" over and over as she slowly made her way to open the door. I would say to myself, "She's thanking God for every step."

I cared for her for 5 years.

During the next 5 years I completed my CNA training and provided skilled care and hospice care. In 2016 I began a private duty case for hospice with Molly. Molly lived upstairs from her niece. I had just completed caring for her niece's husband in the hospice for several months, and now I would be caring for her.

Molly was soft spoken and very thin. She lost her daughter, who had been her primary caregiver. Molly needed assistance with safely transferring from the bed to the walker, and from the walker to her reclining chair.

I provided some light cleaning for her and some cooking, too. The entire family was so nice and welcoming. The niece has a little brown dog, very friendly and loving. Whenever I come in from downstairs, he would come towards me running. I nicknamed him Killer, because he would always lick me to death.

I worked more than one case at a time, so I was also doing a live-in case. One such case was John. Johnny loved baseball and Dean Martin. He needed total care.

One weekend I went home and was relaxing, just watching TV, when I felt a sharp, burning pain across my face and neck. The pain ran all the way down into my hand. It felt like acid burning my skin. It burned and burned and seemed to go on forever. Half of my face went numb.

Once the pain ended, I was so scared, I thought I'd had a stroke. I drove myself to the hospital. In the Emergency Room the doctor said I needed to go to a neurology doctor. The neurology doctor told me I had MS (MS multiple sclerosis). He didn't tell me much else.

I didn't tell my clients. I figured they had enough to think about and didn't want them to worry they might be losing me. I didn't want them to be concerned.

Ever so slowly the feeling came back to my hand and my face. I am now able to care for my clients without pain or fatigue.

And I can even laugh with them at the silly things they say on TV, as I did as a child with Mr. Willie and Miss Ophelia, Mrs. Boswell and Mr. Croffet, and all the neighbors from long ago.

My Journey to Care
PAMELA KAPLAN

A Connecticut native, Pamela Kaplan has been a PCA in private care for over 20 years. "Patience and kindness" are her words to live by. She continues to take training workshops so she can keep up to date with current approaches to patient care and well-being. She believes highly in 'aging in place' and keeping her patients in their home environment where they feel loved and safe. Her family is her cherished 33-year-old son and her two darling bulldogs. She enjoys going camping and attending concerts and film festivals.

I've always been a certain kind of caregiver. I began my journey of care when I was young and always looking out for others that needed help, especially, helping my grandmother with chores.

It continued when I came back from California and my

father's mother, Kathleen Wheeler, aka "Nana," who was in need of a little extra help tending to Grandpa Mike.

Mike was Nana's second husband. I never knew my real grandfather, he passed early in his life from alcoholism.

Grandpa had few words when we were growing up; fewer words when he was diagnosed with dementia. Nana catered to his every need, and it was taking a heavy toll on her.

Now, Nana, she was always on the ball. My best memory is her skill at ironing *everything*. She laundered and ironed all the clothes on Friday so she would be ready for church on Sunday. Oh, she took great care, indeed.

Seeing her struggle, I would bring my son, Zack, when he was five years old at the time, and we would spend the afternoon helping around the house.

Grandpa Mike was always on the run. To see the shell of the man he used to be was disheartening. Despite the dementia, he was a trickster. Mike would hide his pills in the cushion of the kitchen chair. Oh, the way his eyes would light up when he was presented with the evidence, smiling like Mr. Innocent.

Nana cared for him longer than any person could imagine. Finally, she placed him in a nursing home, and he passed a month later.

Well, less than a month after Grandpa Mike passed, Nana came face-to-face with her own health issues. She needed a tracheostomy because of a collapsed windpipe. And soon after that she needed a feeding tube. She spent countless days in the ICU, and then was moved to rehab. After several weeks in rehab, she passed all the criteria for returning to her apartment.

It was a lot to learn for an 82-year-old. But she did it, and she carried on for 3 years. When I say the "roller coaster of life" started, that is no joke.

My brother was a police officer for the town of Waterbury. He would get the call for ambulance assistance at Nana's address and would hustle over there to help her get to the hospital. At the hospital, I would pick up and stay and find out what the issue was this time. There were many Emergency Room visits. It got to the point where we needed to have more assistance, meaning...a nursing home for Nana.

Through all of these trials, I learned how to clean and insert a trach, how to flush the tube after a feeding, and how to keep an elderly person clean and safe from bedsores. I would watch the physical therapists and repeat the exercises at home with her. But let me tell you, that didn't stop Nana from looking fabulous, or even from cooking for my son and me.

Now, just her watching us eat was really hard for me, because I knew all she really wanted was to taste the coffee again and eat a cold devil dog. I loved her for that, even as it broke my heart.

So it came to time for her to move. She accepted it like a champ. Fingers crossed, we found a place that would suit her needs. She spent a week at that facility, but then she moved to another. There were issues with the staff cleaning her trach and suctioning her properly.

Sometimes, when I came to visit I found her with no trach in place at all. They had even left the breakfast tray piled up, with no help to her to eat them.

We moved Nana to another home, and the third one was the charm.

She was tired when she passed. I told her it was ok. She waited until we left the room and that was ok, too.

After Nana was gone I started my journey of being the voice for the helpless, sometimes just being there to hold a hand, to say, "I am here for you, you are okay."

Through the years I have helped my other grandmother, Gammie. And I helped grandfather Bump. I started working with a family in Simsbury, helping mom raise 3 girls. It brought me to their grandmothers and 15 years of caregiving for that family.

Oh, and guess what: I met someone and instantly clicked with his mom, Doris, but that, my friend, is another story, you'll have to wait awhile to hear it.

Through my years of giving care, I have learned to be kind. To be patient. To give someone that calmness that they need right at that moment.

Having that knowledge has given me a fulfilling life.

The Lost Dream

ESMINE MARTIN

Esmine Martin has been a dedicated CNA for over 30 years, and she is known for her compassionate caregiving approach, her smile, and dependability. Her expertise is working with the geriatric population in the dementia unit. Esmine has been a valued mentor to many, many new CNAs over the decades. She is a Christian woman who many residents come to for spiritual comfort. She is very active in her church, and she is also a Trustee. Esmine loves gardening and cooking, and she especially loves babysitting her grandniece.

As a young girl in the early seventies, I was still living in Jamaica with a distant relative. This lady was considered my guardian. She was medium height and build, in her mid-50s. She was always busy and when she got home from work, she was always taking care of her beautiful flower garden. Her name was Josephine Allen. Josephine's mother was very sick, and apparently, she had a major stroke and was unable to walk and talk. Her mother lived with other relatives before, but moved in with Josephine when she became very sick. At that time, I was about 16 years old, and my duty in the home was to take care of the home, Josephine, and her two young sons. I was very reliable and industrious. Eventually, her mother became part of my duty.

My guardian was a single mother and could not afford to pay for outside help. Her mother's nickname was "Mamma Tat." Her real name was Miss Hattie. She was a very pleasant old lady in her mid-eighties. Although she couldn't talk, she could mumble a few words. When things were going well, she would smile; otherwise, she would just sit and stare, looking spaced out.

My guardian was a schoolteacher, and she had a very busy schedule with school duties, as well as with her choir practice. She didn't have to worry about her mom's care; she knew that I was reliable and trustworthy to take care of her mother. I would make sure that Miss Hattie had her bed-bath, her hair combed, and all other aspects of her hygiene care done. She trusted me because I was very gentle when caring for her. When she was comfortable, she would smile. I would feed her three meals each day with her food crushed and liquids thickened. Usually, I would sit patiently when I was doing this. When she was eating or drinking something that she liked, she would smile; otherwise, she shook her head if she disliked something. During this process,

I would talk to her, although she could not respond, she understood.

Doing all this as a young girl, I developed a passion to become a nurse. I tried very hard in Jamaica, but I was unsuccessful. I tried getting into several RN programs, but I did not get through, so I became a practical nurse in Jamaica. I was able to assist in the delivery of a beautiful baby girl, and her mother named her Meisha Gaye. In the eighties, before migrating to the United States, I also got a job where I worked in a doctor's office, where I assisted in taking care of young children.

In the late eighties, I came to the United States. I did home care for a while, and overtime, I became a trained certified nurse's aide (CNA). At that time, I was a broke church mouse, but God has been good to me. While I was in training to become a CNA, I was working at the same facility. I received my first pay and was very excited. My experience of taking care of Miss Hattie helped me and energized me and inspired me to be a wonderful caregiver. I received many certificates and awards for my outstanding performance. I loved my job. I worked at a few nursing homes, both non-union and union, and I am still there after nearly 40 years. I love what I do, and I see it as a blessing every day. It can become very challenging sometimes, but my good faith and patience carry me through.

I had many sisters. One of my favorite sisters recently passed, and every time I think about her and the good times we had growing up as little girls, it brings tears to my eyes. At times, I catch myself and think of the jokes and laughter that we usually had. While my sister was laying on her sick bed, I gave her tender loving care, and I helped her children and other family members to prepare nice meals for her. Her sickness brought me back to the days when I used to take care of Miss Hattie.

My sister passed away peacefully. Looking at my sister on the day of her funeral, I was very sad, even though I put on my best face, my heart was sore inside. Her beautiful casket was surrounded with beautiful flowers and pictures of her and the family, which partially uplifted my spirit.

My dear sister holds a special place in my heart. I still have some unanswered questions for her even though my questions will never be answered. She was my guidance and spiritual leader. May her soul forever rest in peace.

Although I didn't make it to become a nurse here in the United States, I gave myself credit for becoming a wonderful caregiver, and I enjoyed working with some wonderful nurses and co-workers. So, my lost dream has inspired me to become an affluent caregiver. I am a commendable, kind, caring, and thoughtful caregiver.

At her funeral, I was asked to read her obituary, and I happened to crack a few of her jokes. She had a contagious laugh, which drew people towards her. Knowing that I gave my sister the best care, I looked at her in her casket with all the beautiful flowers around her. She was looking so pleasant, and it seemed as if she were smiling at me just like Miss Hattie would smile when I was caring for her.

You see, I know that I may not have become a registered

nurse, the job I thought was my dream, but I do have my dream job of caring for people I love, and I know that my sister is joyful, seeing that I am on my journey care.

Growing Up in Jamaica

LURLETTE NEWELL

Lurlette Newell has worked in the healthcare field for 32 years in the same nursing facility, first in housekeeping and then as a dedicated CNA for nearly 25 years. She worked with behavioral residents, and her specialty was working with dementia patients. Lurlette loved and respected all her residents and was known for her empathy and compassion. The residents in the Home always said that they waited for her every day and rushed to say hello. She has one son who is a Lieutenant in the Department of Corrections. Currently retired, Lurlette enjoys going shopping, going to the movies, walking, writing, and traveling.

Growing up in Jamaica, I was raised by my adorable, beautiful grandmother, who was like a treasure to me. She was humble and kindhearted. She treated me in a

49

very unique way. There are special things that she had done for me. She taught me many lessons in life.

I can remember one day when I was 6 years old, my grandmother was calling for me when I was playing outside with some boys who were my cousins. To be honest, I heard her, but I was too busy having fun with the boys. Eventually, I said to my cousins, "Mum is calling me, and I have to go."

When I went to her, she asked me where I was. I told her that I was riding the coconut bunker with the boys. A coconut bunker is a big limb that fell from a coconut tree and dried. It was so big that we could sit on it and push on it and ride it down a hill. It is like a bobsled, but with no snow.

She raised her hand and said to me, "I told you not to go riding with them." She told me that I was so stubborn. "Why don't you *listen*?" she asked.

Eventually, she held my hands. I knew that she was not going to spank me, but I screamed, knowing that my uncle would come over to ask her what she was doing to me. When he came over, he asked her what she was doing to me. She said to my uncle, "You know that you just have to hold your hand up, and she would scream." She then let me go, and she told me what to do. She smiled at me and told me that I need to listen, and I will get through life. I learned many lessons in listening.

My grandmother taught me how to be respectful to others no matter who they are and to always say good-day to them with a smile—even the dog that is on the street– and she reiterated, "Don't ever forget that," saying that with a smile on her face and full of love. I lived by her example because she was humble and kind and respectful and loving. My grandmother taught me so much. Because of her and through her example, I became a care giver to the elderly.

Coming to the U.S. in 1992, I started in the healthcare field as a housekeeper, then I became a certified nursing assistant in 2000. I became a CNA because I saw how my grandmother treated people with compassion, and she was always there for her family and friends. She always was so kind. I always wanted to be just like her. I wanted to give loving care especially to the elderly.

When I go to work, I always remember my grandmother. I can remember one morning when I went to work, I saw a resident who reminded me of my grandmother. Her name was Martha. I knocked on her door, and I asked her if I could come in. Martha said, "Yes." I said, "Good morning, how was your night? I am here to take care of you." I asked her what she would like me to do for her. She told me, and I said, "We will do that together." We started to do her care together. When we were finished, she gave me a hug, and she said, "Thank you. You are special. And I want you to come see me every morning because you are extra special, and you take wonderful care of me. I love you." I gave her another hug, and said I love you, too, because you remind me of my grandmother.

My grandmother was very petite, and Martha was petite and slender with soft, silky flowing gray hair just like my grandmother's. I looked forward every day to take care of Martha. She loved our walks outside and our special talks. We talked about our families and how much she loved her husband. She always invited me to her birthday party at work, and I became like a member of her family. She was so dear to me, and we did so much together.

Martha was now in her late eighties, and she started to feel a bit sickly, but she never complained. One day, we were so happy talking together at lunch, but she did not want to eat much that day. The nurse checked her, and her vitals were good. Later that afternoon, I walked her to her room so she could lay down. I covered her and sang to her. She went to a peaceful sleep. Before I left my shift, I went to see her and gave her a kiss. She opened her eyes briefly and she knew I was there. She was resting comfortably. That was the last night I saw her. I am so glad I gave her a loving kiss. She passed away in her sleep that night. I write this story in loving memory of Martha.

The Birds

LURLETTE NEWELL

The birds are chirping,

The wind is howling,

The flowers are blooming, and

The sun is shining.

The leaves on the trees are singing.

Smile, be joyful, it is a new day!

Life is a treat, let us live it to the best.

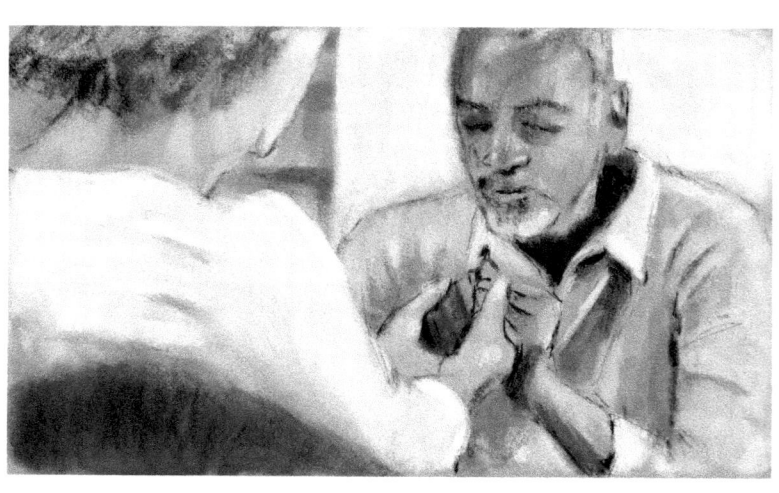

My Life Story

KATHERINE JONES NEWTON

Katherine Jones-Newton is a dedicated PCA with over 12 years' experience in home healthcare in Wallingford, CT. She works with the elderly with extreme health care challenges. She has followed in her mother's footsteps in working in the nursing field. Katherine loves her work and is dedicated to giving exceptional care, respect, and dignity to her clients. She was previously a CNA for 4 years and then a teacher's aide for 6 years working with children ages 3 to 5. But her calling was to be a PCA to take care of the elderly who needed her care and expertise. Katherine's daughter has followed in her footsteps and is a CNA. In her spare time, Katherine loves reading, going to church, and relaxing watching TV.

Growing up as a little child, I remember being so sick that I couldn't do anything at all due to my physical challenges. I could not do the things like the other kids due to my heart problem. As the years went by,

I sat on the porch and watched people and kids doing different activities. I vividly remember the kids in the neighborhood jump roping, roller skating, playing hopscotch, and riding their bikes. And I couldn't. I couldn't jump rope, roller skate, ride a bike, go bowling, or run and do exercises.

From the age of 9 years to 12 years old I felt different and so left out. I cried often. I thought that I would never be able to do things like the other kids. But I had friends who came every week to visit with me. We talked and talked, and they always told me, "Things will get better." I felt better because they cared about me.

When I was a teenager, I began to get better, and I was able to do what other kids could do. I was so thankful that my health returned. I decided that when I finished school, I wanted to be a CNA or PCA or a home care worker. This was important to me because I wanted to help others, especially the elderly, to do things they need to do but could not complete on their own, like me as a child. So, I went to school to become a PCA, and then I took the course to become a CNA.

First, I went to work with the elderly in their homes. Then I went to work in the hospital as a CNA. I loved being a CNA, but I really loved being a home healthcare worker more, because in homecare I could do more for my clients, like being their company, making sure they eat, and taking them outside to get the wonderful sunshine and some walking exercise.

Providing homecare makes me feel good, I can do things for them that I could not do for myself when I was young. I feel that I bring the sunshine with me to work, and maybe a little happiness, too. This is such an important job! I feel that I am helping to inspire my elderly clients and motivate them to do more for themselves.

I love the pay rate that I earn. That being said, I am glad that I work in this field, as I meet all kinds of people in all kinds of shapes and forms. Somedays, I find myself crying because it brings back memories of when I couldn't do those things for myself when I was sick. I was lucky back then that my Godmother was there for me to inspire me to get better. She was heaven-sent just for me! I thank God for my parents, too, for being there at home and being so patient with me.

Now, I can do everything for myself, so if you get sick, do not give up, keep going. I thank God for all of these things that I can do now, not only for myself, but for my clients. Most of all, I feel that it is a privilege and an honor to work in the healthcare field with older people and take care of them.

So there, you see my life story. I thank God for the training that I had to become a PCA, a homecare worker. I found out there are people who are worse off than I was as a child, and they cannot do any of the things I can do now for myself. You see, I was one of the lucky ones who had a chance to become a caring PCA to work with the elderly. I know that due to my childhood challenges, I learned the true meaning of caring, giving, and loving others.

I Am Here to Serve

EMELINE PERALTE

Emeline Peralte is a CNA with over 11 years of experience in nursing home care. She worked for 9 years in the state of New York, then 2 years in Connecticut. Emeline is from Haiti, where she earned a Master's Degree in Doctor of Pharmacy in 1988. Once Emeline moved to the United States, she did not have the immediate opportunity to obtain her Pharmacy degree. Therefore, she chose a career as a Certified Nursing Assistant, which enabled her to use her passion to give care to the elderly population.

With her compassionate caregiving approach, she feels that "The key to success is teamwork." Emeline finds it easy to use her skills, her empathy, her heart, and her strength to improve her patients' well-being. She is a mother of two, and she is Christian member of her community Baptist Church. In her spare time, Emeline likes to read, listen to the news, cook for her family and friends, and help people in need.

From 2012, the time that I choose to become a caregiver, I didn't understand how tough it was. I didn't realize there is a big difference between the theory and the practice. In the real field, we work with real people, not just theory.

At first, when I became a caregiver, I was always feeling nervous and did not know where to start because I was dealing with different people and different cases. There's no way to step back because care is needed; support is necessary. I know I must intervene and do something. There is a routine at work that must be done.

The key to success is "teamwork." To find that, it is not easy all the time, but working as a team is very important. Personally, I found or experienced that when I used my skills, my compassion, my heart, my strength, and my best to achieve, caregiving is easy. God always provides me with the ability to work with another worker, head nurse, or supervisor. With a positive attitude and humor, I'm here to serve, and I have no regrets.

Fiesty Cindy

JOVAN JONES PERRY

Jovan Jones Perry has been a housekeeper at the Hebrew Center Nursing Home in West Hartford for several years. Jovan cares a great deal about the residents in the home, taking the time to listen to their stories and let them know they are honored and loved.

I enjoy caring for others.

Even for a client like Cindy.

Cindy was a client in the nursing home where I work as a housekeeper. She always stayed in her room and to herself. She had a lot of mouth (bad words and sarcasm), and she was not a fan of new people. With new people frequently coming in to care for her, she became more and more agitated and hard to deal with.

I was quiet and only came in to do my work. She noticed that, and one day she mentioned to me that she liked how I am. "Just doing your job and minding your business." I thanked her, and she said I reminded her of her grandson. Our days went from "good morning" and "goodbye" to her telling me about her day and of the fond memories she had about her life. We'd talk for at least 10-15 mins a day. Pretty soon, other staff members noticed that she'd taken a liking to me more than her nurse's aide or RN.

There were times Cindy would refuse her meds. I would mention to her that she needed the medications to live longer and to remain vibrant and healthy. She would turn to the nurse and say, "Okay, give it to me."

There were also times where she was just stubborn and wasn't willing to take her meds, regardless of what anyone said.

Cindy became family to me. I would bring her in something from the avenue for lunch sometimes when she was tired of the food at the home, (with the nurse's approval, to be sure). Even when I was at home sometimes, I would start thinking about what she was doing or who she was cussing out, lol.

"Don't start yo sh*t!"

"Get the hell out of my room!"

"I don't give a damn!"

Those are just a few of the vernacular that she enjoyed spewing.

She was obnoxious and rude, yes, but once she opened up to you, she was warm and considerate. One Friday, she made a joke. The words I remember her saying last are, "They'll have to carry me out of here first." We both laughed, and I said, "I'll see you Monday."

She replied, "Yes, you will."

When I came in to work Monday, Nurse Beth told me Cindy passed over the weekend. It was heartbreaking. She had become family to me.

I will miss her dearly, cuss words and all!

Love Always Remains
LAINA JEAN-PIERRE

Laina Jean-Pierre has worked at Cassena Care of Stamford, Connecticut as a CNA for 19 years. She works with dementia residents, where she brings love, exceptional care, and honesty working with her beloved patients. Laina was a teacher of young children in her home country, Haiti. When she came to the United States, she decided to use her teaching skills to work with adults with dementia, and she became a certified nursing assistant. She earned her United States high school diploma in 2008, and she continued her education at Norwalk Community College and graduated with EKG and phlebotomy certification. Her son graduated with his BSRN, and he is now working as a registered nurse at Yale Hospital. Her daughter graduated with her BS in business administration. Laina's hobbies are cooking, dancing, and listening to Haitian music.

I have been a patient care assistant for the past nineteen years. Recently, I had a patient on my job who passed away, and his passing made me so very sad.

I remember every time I had to give him his AM care, bathing and dressing and getting him out of bed, he always said to me, "Thank you, Laina." And he said it with great passion.

His name was Mr. Alvin Sherfield. He liked to eat salad. He would munch on a carrot like a rabbit. And he loved a grilled cheese sandwich. He drank his coffee black with three sugars! And he could sit for hours watching the TV news, although I'm not sure he understood everything that was being reported.

Mr. Sherfield was a tall man, very friendly, and he liked to laugh a lot, especially when I used to ask him about his past.

I remember he had a pretend girlfriend on the floor. A "Miss Potter." He was always talking about her. And at the same time, there was another "girlfriend," Miss Sorenso, located to another floor! He was always talking about her, too. Sometimes I think he really believed in them.

When I wanted to make him laugh, I would say to him, "You know, Mr. Sherfield, I like Miss Sorenso better than the one in this floor.

He would answer me in the most serious way, "Oh, Laina, you're going to put me in trouble with Miss Potter!"

"I said to him, "No, not *really*."

He looked at me and said, "Laina, you know I love you best of all."

"I said, "I love you, too."

Anyway, Mr. Sherfield left behind a lot of memories.

He was always talking to his mother about me, telling her how I always gave him such good care.

It made me proud.

One day he said to me, "Laina, I am serious, I don't know what I will be doing without you, because you are so good to me." He was scheduled to go into the hospital, you see, for a procedure. It was 7:30 in the morning. I washed him up, dressed him and did everything he needed.

When it was time for him to go, I have him a big hug. And a kiss on the top of his bald head.

He looked at me and said, "Laina, I love you."

I answered him, "I love you, too."

It was the last conversation we had together. The last time we looked into each other's eyes with love and affection, for he passed away in the hospital and I never saw him again.

But he is with me in spirit, and will be, always. For love always remains.

The Journey of the Unknown

JARITZA RIVERA

Jaritza Rivera has been a devoted PCA for the past 20 years, but she actually began her healthcare journey as a teenager taking care of her ailing parents. Her caring and generous nature and her devotion to helping others led to her recent enrollment in LPN school. She is a diligent worker and committed to reaching her personal and professional goals. As an LPN, she will continue to give exceptional healthcare, respect, and support to her patients and their families. Also, Jaritza has been an 1199 SEIU New England Union delegate for about 3 years, and she strongly advocates for union members. She is also very involved in many community activities. In her spare time, she loves to read and write in her journal, and she has a special love and respect for nature.

I was washing my mom's hair one day, lathering her curls with her favorite lavender-smelling shampoo, when I realized she wasn't as physically mobile as she used to be.

At the doctor's appointment we received the news that mom had multiple diagnoses: diabetes, high blood pressure, and cancer of the uterus. These infirmities were disabling and making it impossible for her to take care of herself.

I now had to change my work and take care of mom, which became difficult as more test results came back and more medical problems developed. It was an uphill battle as we began the journey of the unknown.

Life became difficult for us both, since mom was the patient and I, her daughter. We had to face the fact that we would now need a lot of physical, mental and emotional support for both of us.

My mother's name is Sonia Ortiz. She stands a big five feet, one inch high, a tough and strong little cookie. She is truly the strongest person I know. In my eyes she has always been my role model...and my hero!

Now I feel I am hers, helping her continue to strive with her health issues, helping her with small exercises, keeping her as healthy as possible, even in the toughest times.

As her daughter and caregiver, I am happy to spend this time getting closer to her, and she, growing closer to me. Bringing joy to my heart while also maintaining a positive, feel-good emotion as we continue this difficult journey. Realizing that staying positive isn't always easy in tough times, but it is highly needed.

For mother and daughter.

An Inspirational Moment
PATRICIA ROBINSON-POWELL

Patricia Powell worked with the Visiting Nurses Association for 6 years, and then she came to Arden House, which is a nursing facility in Hamden, CT. There, she has happily worked in the housekeeping department for the past 7 years. Patricia loves being able to collaborate daily with the residents. She plans to go back to school to become a recreational therapist. She has three grown children, whom she loves to spend time with. She loves to sing in the gospel choir of her church and teach people how to pray. She is also an avid traveler.

A moment that inspired me was when I worked as a home health aide, and I worked with a patient who lived at home. I worked with an agency, and I was sent to this new patient for the first time. Her name was

Donna, and she was about 75 years old. Donna was a tiny, white woman, who was very frail and afraid to go outside. She had one son, but he didn't really care about her. When I started to work for Donna, she just stayed in her room, and she prayed her Rosaries and smoked her cigarettes. Donna was a devoted Catholic.

Every morning when I came to Donna's house, she would cheerfully say, "Is that you Patty-Ann?" That was her nickname for me. She didn't like going outside or even walking around her own home. She was depressed and lonely because she had few visitors. and her son never came to visit her. I was hurt and felt so bad for her, so my soon-to-be husband, Jerry and I became her family.

Donna had several doctors and nurses due to her debilitating cancer. Donna could not do much on her own so that meant that I was to go to the stores, pay her bills, or go to the bank for her. Jerry and I would cook for her. Whenever I brought my lunch, she wanted my lunch, so I always packed a lunch for two. Jerry is a very good cook. Donna loved his lunches.

During the day, we watched TV. She especially liked the Catholic church station. We talked about everything together. She told me about her time as a nun. She told about her holidays, and that she would send her son money, but he never responded or even said, "Thank you." When I heard this, it made me sad, and I wanted to tell her to stop sending him money, but that was not my place. Donna appreciated that I was a good listener.

After working with Donna for about a year, she started

to come out of her room more often to sit in the living room with me. She began talking with me more. This made both of us happy. Donna enjoyed the kindness, caring, and respect I showed to her. She also trusted me so much that she wanted only me to take care of her and take care of her financial matters. I felt very privileged that she trusted me to that extent. I was able to get Donna to go to her doctor appointments more easily, and that made me feel good. She started eating in the kitchen, and we began talking about God and how much she loved my husband to be, Jerry. Jerry would often come to visit her with me. We were her family!

One day, Donna had to go to the hospital. She fell, and I found her on the floor in her bedroom. I went with her in the ambulance to keep her calm and let her know I was there for her. The doctors sent her to a nursing home, which she did not like. Donna called me to come to the nursing home. She and I talked to her social worker. A week later, Jerry and I went to the nursing home and brought her back home. We were all relieved and glad she was in her own home.

Weeks later, Donna fell again, but this time it was more serious. She went back to the hospital, but her doctors sent her to Yale for Hospice care. I saw her every day, but she was getting weaker and weaker. She began talking to me about her desired funeral and burial arrangements. Not long before, her dog died, and she had him cremated. She requested that her beloved dog be placed with her in cremation. I would hold her hand, and I prayed with her. This was so difficult seeing her fade away. Jerry and I were to be married in a few weeks, and we so very much wanted Donna at our wedding. Donna passed away just days before our wedding.

Donna was loved, and she inspired me to continue showing my care to other clients. She respected and trusted me so much. I came to feel like her daughter. She inspired my strength to carry on serving my clients with the utmost care, kindness, and respect. Most importantly, she taught me patience, listening skills, and to continue to keep my family close and dear to me. I was glad to be able to do so much for Donna, and I will never forget her. I love her for all she did for me.

I'm On My Way!

MARIBEL RODRIGUEZ

Maribel Rodriguez worked as a CNA for 30 years in a Waterbury, CT nursing home. While working in the Home she became involved with the 1199 NE union issues. When she left the nursing home Maribel worked for the union full time. Her responsibilities included nursing home organizing, preparing them for strikes and other job actions, and educating members about the importance of being involved in state political issues. She is now happily retired and enjoying her three children and four grandchildren.

"Hi, Deb, I'm on my way! I will be there in ten minutes!"

As I was driving, I was thinking how important this election is! How can people believe a candidate that spins lie after lie? Whatever happened to character and integrity!

Before I realized it, I was in front of her house, a gray,

well-kept cottage with a beautiful bay window. I can see all the beautiful plants in the window.

Deb has a beautiful smile and curly thick hair with streaks of gray. She is a woman that unapologetically makes her opinion known. I love her straightforward attitude and how she makes me laugh.

As she gets in the car she says, "I'm really afraid! Girl, we have to stop that man from getting into the office." "It's like watching The Handmade Tales," I reply. "Our rights are being taken away."

"If he gets in again we won't have the right to vote! I'm really afraid!"

As we came to a light and are stopped I said, "I don't understand why some people don't realize our democracy is in danger. He said he likes Putin! Can you believe it? I know he's a dangerous man. He's Facist!"

She said, "I know. And he met the guy from North Korea!!"

I said, "That's why we're knocking on doors of union members today and talking to them about what's at stake!"

As we pulled up to the democratic office to get our lists, Deb said, "Let's do this!"

"And while we are doing it, we will get some exercise!" I said.

Deb added, "Yeah, and we even have a beautiful sunny day to be out meeting our neighbors!"

Stay tuned!

Pardon Me If I Get Emotional

MARK SANOGUEIRA

Mark Anthony SaNogueira is currently a PCA with a client in the New Haven area. He is blessed with four children, five grandchildren and five step grandchildren. Mark is widowed from his second wife. He enjoys helping those that need care. Seeing happy children gives him the greatest joy.

I have no idea what I'm doing.

I always wanted to write, but I always thought that what I had to say wasn't important enough. I was told that I am wrong to even try. But everyone has something important to say, if they can just find the courage to put their words down on paper.

I have been a PCA for less than a year. I have only had one client (so far). So let me tell you about her.

Roberta is partially disabled. She can walk, but only in

short segments. There are also some emotional issues. She seems very high strung, but inside I am sure there is a heart of gold.

It took me a while to realize that I need to be patient with her. There are so many things that I may or may not be aware of that make her act the way she does.

I wonder if she feels the same about me. Does everyone go through this?

Probably so.

Roberta, my client is a good cook. She makes a really good chicken parm. I can smell it cooking while I'm working. I don't care that much for red sauce at a restaurant, but there is nothing like home made. Roberta's is pretty awesome, although nothing beats mom's. She comes from an Italian family.

Roberta's strongest point is that she doesn't take "No" for an answer. For example, if there is something wrong in her apartment, she calls maintenance and has a lengthy conversation with them. If the problem isn't resolved immediately, she is on the phone with the city. If *that* doesn't work, she contacts someone on the State level. They usually start listening then.

Her persistence almost always pays off.

I told her she should have been a reporter, laugh-out-loud. But her persistence is also her weakest point. She tends to alienate people, keeping her circle of friends very small. I, on the other hand, try to befriend everyone, making me vulnerable to being used.

Roberta is also a good Christian. I was born and raised

Roman Catholic. I don't practice my faith much, but I still believe, and I pray a lot.

I must confess, I was mad at God for a bit. He took my wife from me. Monica (my late wife) was a saint. She didn't use her condition (Multiple Sclerosis) as a crutch. In fact, she blossomed into a very successful Tupperware director. This woman was on the phone constantly. Not just for Tupperware, but for helping friends that had reached out to her. I still get messaged to this day from folks saying what an inspiration she was to them.

I soon realized that being mad at God was selfish, because Monica was no longer in pain. I needed her, but I think God must have needed her more. She was an angel on earth and now she must be one in heaven.

I enjoy being a PCA because if enables me to help someone, and it makes me feel good about myself.

Don't we all want to feel good about ourselves some time?

I also enjoy working at my friend's carnival. I run a kiddie ride. Easy work, and nothing warms my heart more than a happy child. My children are all grown now and on their own. My grandkids are great, too, but they are growing up too fast for me to keep up. Seeing the little one's on the ride brings back warm memories of my past. My therapist says these things that make me happy are good for me (laugh-out-loud).

I won't be on this earth forever, so I plan on getting the most enjoyment while I'm here.

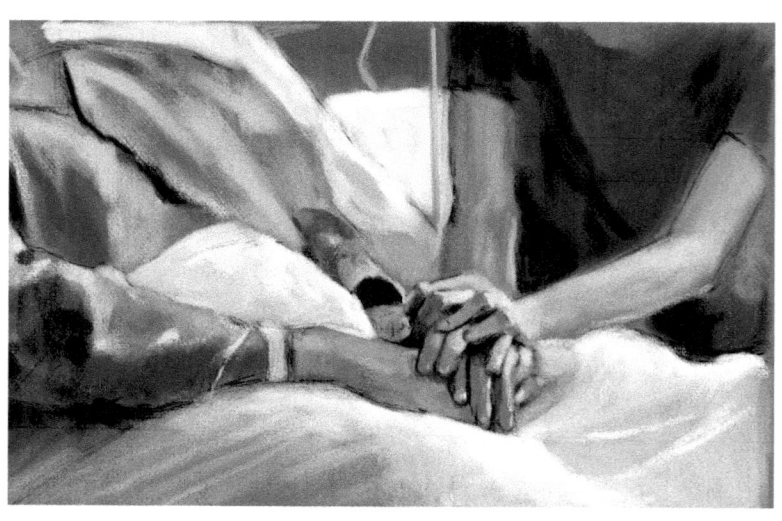

Ken, My Bright Light!
VALMARIE SMITH

Born in Tobago (Trinidad & Tobago) in the Caribbean, Valmarie migrated to the United States over 40 years ago. She worked as a CNA for over 25 years in the same facility and has a lifetime of experiences as a result. Now retired, her number one passion is reading...and writing! She currently resides in Connecticut, where she volunteers in the READ Program for the public schools.

My encounter with the medical field was quite by accident. I accompanied a friend who was applying for a job and decided to submit an application of my own. Lo and behold, I was hired. This was my first time in the medical field. I was a graduate of the first certified nursing assistant class in the state of Connecticut. That was in 1983. Since then, it has been quite a journey with lots of amazing experiences, an eye opener and a learning journey.

One experience stands out vividly. One of my residents, Ken, came to my facility in Manchester, Connecticut, from Pennsylvania after being in an auto accident. He became blind and partially handicapped. At times, he would become so frustrated because he was so used to being independent, but now he had to adjust to his new way of living. Losing most of his independence, at the young age of 35, made him sad and angry. Ken was a big, burly teddy bear of a guy. He loved to joke and laugh and tell stories. He made me and the staff laugh. We loved Ken.

At his good moments, we would joke around. He would tell me riddles like, "What does FORD stand for?" When I couldn't answer, he told me it's, "Fix or repair daily." We would laugh, and I would tell him of all the abbreviations like LOL, FOMO, TTYL etc. to keep him up-to-date. We had a good relationship.

At times, Ken would talk about all the silly things that he did growing up. When he told his stories as he reminisced, he would have a glow of happiness on his face. Oh, we would have great talks at times. Sometimes, though, he would get totally angry and out of control, especially when he was in the common lounge area, where most of the other residents gathered for activities. He would get disturbed and bewildered over the different sounds and noises that he heard because he couldn't see or move around as he was accustomed to doing. He didn't know what was going on. He would shout in anger. Everyone in the room could feel the hushed uneasiness and become silent.

Whenever I was around, the only thing that would

calm Ken down was my singing to him because I was always singing on the job. The funny thing is, my voice is not great. I grew up with my grandmother, whose voice wasn't good either. She sang all the time...I got this from her.

When Ken got in an angry mood and had outbursts, I would get close behind his chair and softly and gently start singing in a slow and whispering voice in his ear. When I began to sing, you could actually see him start to relax and slowly perk up. He would rock his head from side to side to the beat and would begin to sing with me.

Our favorite song was "Sunshine on My Shoulders Makes Me Happy." Before long, he would be laughing and he would begin to sing his next favorite song, which was "Mustang Sally." He loved that song because he loved cars. Everyone in the room saw his change of demeanor as he became happier. Everyone would join in the sing-along, and before long, the whole world would seem like a happier place.

So, whenever Ken would get out of control, if I was at work, the staff would say, "Go get Val so she can sing to him!"

If Ken and I were sitting around in the dining room or lounge area with other staff members, I would draw him into our circle and into any conversations that we were having because he loved to be included. Ken was a great conversationalist, and he always had so much to add to our lively conversations.

Ken was a truly unique and special person. He would

always tell me, "Val, you are my best buddy." He meant that, which made me feel good, too! I have learned so much from him by seeing his daily struggles to accept, adapt, and find joy in his new lifestyle. It is very hard to be dependent on others when you are so used to being independent. I was lucky to have met and worked with Ken. He was a bright light in my life. Wouldn't you say?

My Son

ELSIE M SOLIS

After working in different companies doing different jobs, I decided to go to a Technical School, where I graduated as a Health Claims Specialist. But because I could not find a place or person who could take care of my children and did not have money to pay for their care, I decided to apply to the Wal-Mart company, where they offered me an overnight schedule. The children's father would take care of them at night, and I would care for them during the day. The shift work was very difficult, but I completed 19 years of work there. I continued working the overnight shift 3 days a week, and 7 days a week I work as a PCA at my son's house. My children today are all good people and are examples of honesty and good values. Two of them served in the United States Army.

In my spare time I love sewing. During the year of COVID 19, I managed to sew more than 1,000 masks to send to Puerto Rico because there was a shortage. I like to write poems, which I share with my children and friends.

When my son Jairo Emmanuel was in high school he was a very fast runner. He finished first in his race. I was so proud of him. He was always an independent person who had his own take on life. He was a lucky guy, with beautiful green eyes.

After he graduated from high school, he became a truck driver. He enjoyed going to the gym and riding his motorcycle. He made new friends on the truck driving job, working in Middletown City.

When he was 29 years old, he was still healthy and athletic, with a lot of projects in his life and a lot of plans for his future.

Until the accident.

On that fateful day, I was getting ready to go to work at 3:30 in the morning. My shift was starting at 4:30. Jairo called to let me know that he was returning to rest for a little bit, as he always did, because he had worked an overtime shift due the bad weather condition. He warned me to be careful while driving to work because the roads were very slippery.

Not long afterward a police officer knocked on the door to give me the terrible news: Jairo had been in a car accident. He was taken to General Hospital in Hartford, CT, unconscious and in critical condition. It was the most terrible moment that any mother or father could have, and besides that, I had my daughter and son doing military service far from home.

After 6 months in three different hospitals, he came home with many mental and physical limitations. His vision was limited, he had completely lost his speech, and he and I needed to learn a little bit sign language.

I had to do everything for him, from bathing him, cleaning him and feeding him. It was very difficult. Jairo is 5'10" tall and weighs about 200 pounds, and I'm just 5'1" and weigh 135 pounds.

For the next three years Jairo continued going to speech, physical and body movement therapies three time a week at Gaylord Hospital and the Specialist hospital in New Britain. He was also taken to aquatic therapies.

This is how I entered the PCA program. I received a phone call in June, 2023, where I learned Jairo had qualified for a program to receive help in his daily life, and he could choose the person to help. He selected me as the right person.

Today, Jairo lives alone in his house. Although he cannot walk, he can see clearly, he can speak, although still with difficulty, but quite understandably. He can mostly take care of himself. Up to 75% of the improvement has been excellent, and I give 100% credit to Jairo: he is a very organized, disciplined and tenacious person. Whatever he sets out to do he achieves. He continues doing his physical exercises in his own house gym and is getting stronger by the day.

And each time I see how far he has come, how he has never, *ever* given up, my heart near bursts with pride.

And love.

Peanut Butter And Jelly

TINA STEVENS

Tina Stevens is a wife, mother of two young adults, and a minister in her church. She is a PCA caregiver for a private family, having cared for them for 16 years. Her ministry includes helping others with chores, or just being a good listener.

Kathy and I are just like peanut butter and jelly.

Let me tell you about Kathy. My sister Berta met her at a school when she was a teacher at Stepping Stone School in Westport Connecticut and Kathy was six years old. Berta was getting to know Kathy in school and became very attached to the child.

Kathy's parents saw how beautifully the two of them were getting along, and so they hired Berta for private care at their home.

Berta worked for the family for several years. She

brought Kathy to all my family events. Our whole family soon fell in love with the little girl.

Berta was so happy in her work caring for Kathy, she decided to take up another career as a caregiver. As a result, she could no longer care for Kathy.

I had just lost my job, and Kathy's parents were looking for another care giver for their daughter. So, Berta suggested me for the job because Kathy already knew me and we got along so well.

At first I didn't think I could do the job caring for Kathy, who was now twelve years old, because the child suffered from severe autism. She had a mind of a five-year old. I noticed that Kathy lacked discipline and boundaries. So I, as a praying person, followed my spirit, which would always give me guidance and direction in Kathy's care.

Kathy is now 28 years old today. I have been with Kathy for 16 years of her life, and I love her like she was my own daughter.

She has come a long way from the beginning stages of our relationship. She is talking a little more now, she has learned boundaries, and she has more discipline.

What I've learned about Kathy is, she can read at a 2nd grade level. So I have included reading in our daily routine. I take Kathy shopping and to the malls. Basically, I take her everywhere I go. I don't exclude Kathy from anything I do.

When she has a meltdown in the stores, I get Kathy to focus on me. Sometimes I have to get in Kathy's face to draw her attention on me, and sometimes I have to elevate my voice to keep her focused on me. Once I do that, she comes back to herself and gives me a big hug and a kiss.

Sometimes I make jokes out of her meltdown. When I do that, she is real good after the episode.

Through the years of caring for her, I have learned that not all people understand what Kathy goes through in her day. And to tell you the truth, it's not easy for people outside of her immediate family and caregiver to understand her. She lives in a different kind of world.

I find that with structure, boundaries, discipline and, most of all, love and understanding, Kathy has a well-rounded life.

I do understand that a person on the austism spectrum can enjoy a good life if your care is loving and consistent. You have to mean what you say, and you can't back down on anything, because Kathy looks for the loopholes and will run with that. You have to stay firm to everything you say and do. And change, which is hard for her, will happen if you stick with the plans you have for her.

One thing I have realized in the beginning of this job is, Kathy is very smart. My first summer working for the family, I was in the laundry room doing laundry. The home is a really big house. All of a sudden, a warning came on the TV saying a severe thunderstorm was coming through. Kathy and her dog Fluffy were outside. I made both of them come in the house because there is a pool and a swing set out in the back yard. I knew that lightning strikes metal objects and people in a pool.

Once the child and dog were safe inside, I set the deadbolt lock on the door and went back to the laundry room. While I was folding the laundry, I heard my spirit say to me, "She's not in the house."

I looked all over the house for Kathy.

She was nowhere to be found.

I asked her dog Fluffy to find her. Fluffy went to the back door and scratched at it. Soon as I opened the door, Fluffy went to the bottom of the steps and sat down. I said to him, "Go find Kathy!"

Fluffy ran to the pool. He wiggled underneath the gate and ran to the pool house. I opened the door; there was Kathy lying on the couch.

Kathy is real smart. She had gone to the in-law quarters of the house and climbed out the window. She pulled the window and the screen back down, but she left the blinds up. That was a dead giveaway that she was real smart. She even closed the door to the in-law room to hide what she had done!

Kathy is a tall chunky girl. She has brown hair with blonde streaks. She is sweet when she wants to be and she can be stubborn sometimes and refuse to listen. But we all have those types of days. I love her regardless; the good, the bad and the ugly. My family and I all love her, and she knows it. That's the best part of caring for Kathy.

Changing Lives Matters

ANN MARIE NICOLE VIRGO

Ann Marie Nicole Virgo has been a PCA since 2023. Ann Marie has a special gift for listening to people in need and understanding their suffering. She plans to continue her education and to give her clients the outstanding, loving care that they deserve.

I can remember my mom putting an old lady on a table and giving her a sponge bath. The old lady was fragile, only about 90 pounds, and bed ridden. My mom was a manager at Kentucky Fried Chicken in Brooklyn, NY, but she would take care of this lady one day of the weekend. My mom did a lot of things. The thing that gave her the most joy was taking care of that old lady. While I watched my mom bathe the woman like a child, I thought, to myself, "I'm never doing that kind of work." I was seven years old at that time.

Fast forward, my Aunt Linda, a CNA, called me to take care of her client for two days. I was only 21 at this time. This woman was about the same age as the lady my mom used to take care of. I looked at the lady, and she reminded me of the same old lady that my mom cared for. She was very fragile and weak, and she needed gentle care. I changed the lady's diaper when she woke up. I made her oatmeal with minimal sugar and fed her. I saw that she had books near her bed. I began to read to her until she fell asleep. I left her in her room and walked into the living room to gather my thoughts. At that very moment, I realized that 'I am my mom!' My mom always took us to her jobs. That's how I know how to take care of people.

A friend of mine, who has been in my life for about 35 years, was diagnosed with cancer. Before he knew that he had cancer and had his surgery, I had already been taking care of him as a friend. He was a strong old man, living by himself, but he needed some help around the house. He is a good person, with a kind heart, and I wanted to help him out. So, I did some housework and brought him good home-cooked meals. He always told me how much he loved and appreciated my cooking. I did lots of cleaning around the house, so his mom left recipes in the cabinet, which I found and copied. That is the way I learned some good cooking tips.

After he was diagnosed with types of cancer he needed an operation. He had a laryngoplasty. He was no longer able to speak. Now, I became his official Personal Care Assistant (PCA). I cooked and cleaned for him. In the middle of his sickness, he became disabled. He couldn't walk right; he couldn't stand for long. He couldn't do the things that he used to do. That irritated him tremendously. He began to get frustrated and didn't want to converse with anyone. So, I learned how to speak to him.

I was not trained to deal with speech therapy, but every day, I learned to listen to his words coming out of his mouth. Within three weeks, I could understand everything he was saying. I would repeat what he said so that he would know I understood him. By the time it came for him to talk to others, he was practically whispering. Now, he can talk to his kids and grandkids on a tablet with no problem. I feel it is important for him to eat good food, live in a clean environment, and get fresh air daily. I believe I have improved his quality of life. He is much happier since the surgery. He looks forward to getting out of bed, showering, shaving, and to seeing me when I get to his bedside.

This gentleman, with a kind heart, helped me become more passionate about my work as a PCA. From my perspective now, I do very important work as a personal care assistant, and I have learned to admire the work that mother used to do. I am appreciative that I can work and will put my best foot forward to help make other people's lives better. I will continue to educate myself in this field that I enjoy so much.

Miracle Baby!

TIFFANY MATHIS WILLIAMS

Tiffany Mathis Williams has been a PCA since 2020, and she is her brother's PCA. As a PCA, she brings her special skills of concern, kindness, compassion, and love to take care of her brother, who is on the autism spectrum. She feels that her calling is to take care of and be an advocate for people who need her care and strength and who cannot take care of themselves. Tiffany is a dedicated advocate for the SEIU New England Union, and is a graduate of the Leadership Academy of this Union. At her church, she is a youth and young adult coordinator. She especially enjoys spending time with her son.

I want to express my gratitude to God, who is the ruler of my life, firstly and foremost.

When my brother, Daniel, was born, the doctors said

he would not make it past 2 years old, but we knew who had the final say. Daniel was born a mere two pounds, and he had tubes attached to him for many months to keep him alive. You see, he was born with epilepsy, and he was bed-bound. He has been non-verbal his whole life. To God be the glory that my brother celebrated his 38th birthday on April 2 this year! And, that is God's will.

I had been a major caretaker of Daniel since he was about 13, and I was only 15. I stepped in to take care of my brother because no one knows or understands him better than my family and me. I felt that I was the right person to take care of him. God gave me the strength, courage, and the understanding and the confidence to know I can handle the responsibility to care for my middle brother. He needed someone who loved him to be there for him. If he was sent to a nursing facility, he would not have his family by his side every minute of the day. He had loving care at home, and my family and I were the perfect ones to be by his side. If he was in a facility, he may have gone to heaven by now.

Even though he cannot speak, he knows we are here, he honestly trusts us, and he knows he is loved unconditionally. He is a miracle baby!

As Daniel got older, I had to go to work outside the home. I was a mail sorter for Pitney Bowes in Hartford, CT. When I got home from work, I helped my mother take care of Daniel. It was very frightening to see the daily challenges he went through with his epilepsy. It was hard for me to see his seizures and keep him safe when he was seizing. Basically, because of my love for

Daniel, I wanted to be there for him throughout his journey through life.

I became a mother when I was 27. I now have a 12-year-old son. He loves to play the drums, which he took up when he was only 4. He loves to draw and build his own computer games and play them after he finishes building them. My son loves his Uncle Daniel and is learning how to care for him. He watches me care for and give Daniel his medicine. My son is also involved with and is there for Daniel!

I needed to stop working so that I could do more for my brother. In my late 30s, I began to care full-time for Daniel. I could have done any other kind of work, but I chose to take care of my brother. When he sees me, he is always smiling, and when I see my brother smiling, it is the motivation to keep me doing what I have been doing all my life, which is to provide quality care for him.

One day, one of my cousins was talking with my mother and me, and she said, "Do you know that Tiffany can be paid to work for her sibling, Daniel?" My mother was excited to learn how. My cousin said you can become a Personal Care Assistant, a PCA.

I said, "What? *Really?* How do I sign up to be a PCA?" The reason I was this interested is because I could do more for my brother and have a paid position that would help me survive and take care of my son. So, through the company Allied, I took an orientation through Zoom and obtained the opportunity to become my brother's caretaker. I am proudful that I am still

Daniel's caretaker, but I am also proud that I stand on my own as a PCA, my paid profession.

Caring for someone with epilepsy, who is bedridden and unable to speak, is undoubtedly challenging. However, my dedication and love for my brother shine through, and I am committed to exceeding expectations and making a such a great difference in my brother's life. The support and guidance that I have received from my church and community, particularly my organizer and the 1199 Union, have also been instrumental in shaping my journey as a PCA.

By sharing my story, I am not only expressing my gratitude to God, but also inspiring others who may be facing similar challenges. My faith, resilience, and unchanging love for my brother serve as a testimony to the power of caregiving and the impact it can have on someone's life.

I continue to lean on my faith, and may God bless PCAs in our important roles as caregivers for our consumers. Our commitment and love are truly inspiring.

OTHER STORY COLLECTIONS BY 1199 NE MEMBERS

With Our Loving Hands – 1199 Nursing Home Workers Tell Their Story, 2014.

Caring - 1199 Nursing Home Workers Tell Their Story, 2016.

My Open Heart - 1199 Nursing Home and Homecare Workers Tell Their Story, 2018.

Care Under Covid – District 1199 New England Nursing Home & Home Care Workers Tell Their Story